ESPECIALLY FOR HOPPER
WITH LOTS OF LOVE, GRANDPAT

FOR BRUCE —L. M.

Text © 2009 by J. Patrick Lewis.
Illustrations © 2009 by Lynn Munsinger.

Book design by Molly Baker.
Typeset in Filosophia.
The illustrations in this book were rendered in watercolor.

Library of Congress Cataloging-in-Publication Data
Lewis, J. Patrick.
Spot the plot : a riddle book of book riddles / by J. Patrick Lewis ;
illustrated by Lynn Munsinger.
p. cm.
ISBN 978-0-8118-4668-4
1. Riddles, Juvenile. I. Munsinger, Lynn, ill. II. Title.
PS3562.E9465S76 2009
811'.54—dc22
2008003206

Manufactured by Toppan Leefung, Da Ling Shan Town, Dongguan, China, in August 2011.

10 9 8 7 6 5 4 3 2

This book conforms to CPSIA 2008.

Chronicle Books LLC
680 Second Street, San Francisco, California 94107

www.chroniclekids.com

SPOT *the* PLOT

A RIDDLE BOOK *of* BOOK RIDDLES

by J. PATRICK LEWIS   *illustrated by* LYNN MUNSINGER

chronicle books·san francisco

The sky shook,
the wind tossed
me in the air.
Toto-ly lost,

I came upon
three strangers. We
kept each other
company.

Adventures followed
without pause,
and it was all, well,
just bec-**Oz.**

Being brave
is all about
getting your
appendix out!

Ambulance comes
and takes away
lucky me
from school one day.

But it turns
my classmates blue—
they want an
appendix, too.

**Paris, France,
is where I shine.
Fill me in—I'm
_____!**

This is a hare-raising
book review
about a rabbit
who skipped the stew.

He lost his clothes.
He hurried. He hid.
Oh, the rabbity
things he did.

He's old Mrs. Rabbit's
pickiest eater,
**this naughty bunny
whose name is**

_____.

This poor miss
had two sis-
ters who were
mean to her.
Met a prince.
Ever since
royal balls,
he recalls
maiden who
wore a shoe
made of glass.
Found the lass
with the foot
that she put
into it—
slipper fit!

Dear Friends,

A worldwide hike is what I took
and fell into this picture book
of many mini-shots of me,
though I am very hard to see.

Imagine a castle
without any towers,
or a thundercloud bursting
without any showers.
Now imagine a bull
who loved only flowers.

One day he went wild.
(The cause: **a bee sting!**)
So they brought him to fight
matadors in the ring.
Instead he sat smelling
the flowers of spring.

You can't make a bull
always follow the herd.
The very idea is
completely absurd.

There is a book
I know you know—
the perfect bedtime
book, although

the rabbit who
has gone to bed
can't fall asleep
until she's said

to many of
her closest friends,
Goodnight, **Goodnight**. . . .
And so it ends.

Good
wood
makes
fake
bad
lad.
Toy
boy
cries,
lies.
Nose
grows.

One special train.
One little boy.
One Christmas gift—
not quite a toy:

A reindeer bell
jingling good cheer
that only believers
in Santa hear.

HER HAIR'S THE STAIRS

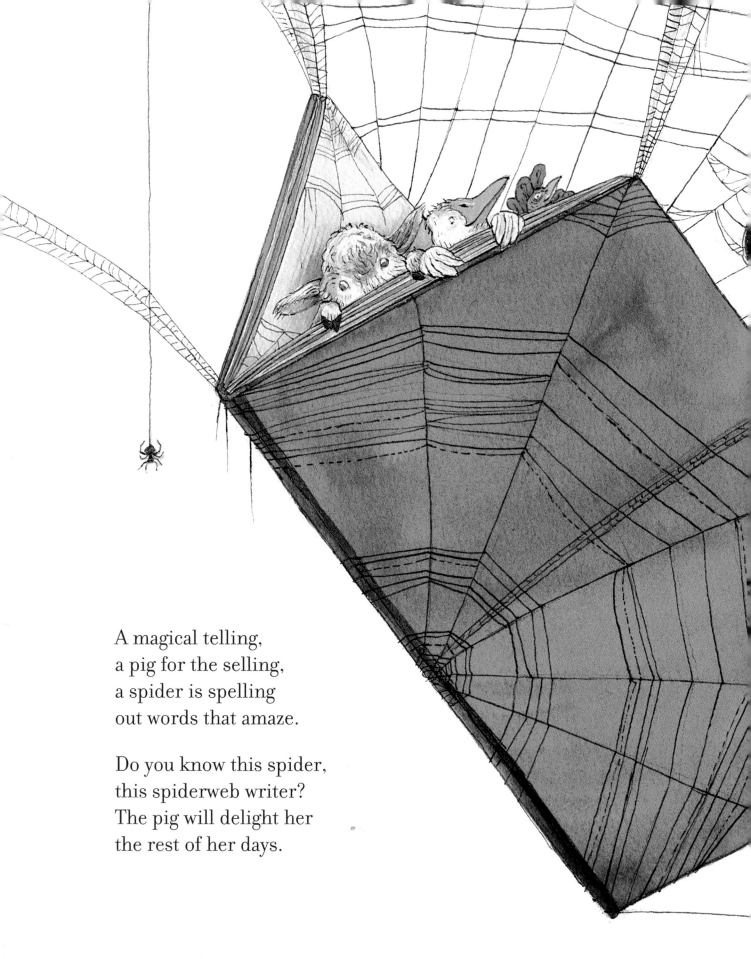

A magical telling,
a pig for the selling,
a spider is spelling
out words that amaze.

Do you know this spider,
this spiderweb writer?
The pig will delight her
the rest of her days.

I'm a penguin, though rather odd.
My penguin friends think I'm a clod.
They march and dive so perfectly,
Sing perfect songs, too (not like me!).
One day some hunters, silly chaps,
Set out some pretty penguin traps,
Though they had not seen such a bird.
I dived a cannonball—absurd!—
And squeaked so far off-off-off-key,
The hunters ran away from me!
My friends agree it's good they found
An odd penguin to have around.

Dear Mr. Farmer,

The letter we're typing
goes under griping!
This barn is too cold,
not climate-controlled.
If we have to shiver,
we don't deliver.
No bedding? No butter.
No blankets? No udder.

Stop the madness.
End the battle.

Sincerely yours,
The Cattle

THE WONDERFUL WIZARD OF OZ
L. Frank Baum

MADELINE * Ludwig Bemelmans

THE TALE OF PETER RABBIT
Beatrix Potter

CINDERELLA * Charles Perrault

WHERE'S WALDO? * Martin Handford

THE STORY OF FERDINAND
Munro Leaf * *illustrated by* Robert Lawson

GOODNIGHT MOON
Margaret Wise Brown * *illustrated by* Clement Hurd

THE ADVENTURES OF PINOCCHIO * Carlo Collodi

THE POLAR EXPRESS * Chris Van Allsburg

RAPUNZEL * The Brothers Grimm

CHARLOTTE'S WEB * E. B. White

TACKY THE PENGUIN
Helen Lester * *illustrated by* Lynn Munsinger

CLICK, CLACK, MOO: COWS THAT TYPE
Doreen Cronin * *illustrated by* Betsy Lewin

the
END